P9-CCT-892

"I didn't wish for anything I couldn't get,
and I got pretty near everything I wanted
because I worked for it."

—Louis Armstrong

Johnny Collins
presents
The International Star
Louis Armstrong
Worlds Greatest Trumpete

Louis Armstrong

By Kindle Fahlenkamp-Merrell

COVER PHOTO

Portrait of Louis Armstrong
© Bettmann/Corbis

Published in the United States of America by The Child's World®, Inc.
PO Box 326
Chanhassen, MN 55317-0326
800-599-READ
www.childsworld.com

Product Manager Mary Francis-DeMarois/The Creative Spark
Designer Robert E. Bonaker/Graphic Design & Consulting Co.
Editorial Direction Elizabeth Sirimarco Budd
Contributors Mary Berendes, Red Line Editorial, Katherine Stevenson, Ph.D.

Library of Congress Cataloging-in-Publication Data
Fahlenkamp-Merrell, Kindle.
Louis Armstrong / by Kindle Fahlenkamp-Merrell.
p. cm.
Includes bibliographical references (p.) and index.
ISBN 1-56766-919-0 (lib. bdg. : alk. paper)
1. Armstrong, Louis, 1901–1971—Juvenile literature. 2. Jazz
musicians—United States—Biography—Juvenile literature. [1. Armstrong,
Louis, 1901–1971. 2. Musicians. 3. Jazz. 4. African
Americans—Biography.] I. Title.
ML3930.A75 F34 2001
781.65'092—dc21

00-013155

Contents

Growing Up

In the 1900s, New Orleans, Louisiana, was one of the most unusual cities in the country. People from many backgrounds lived there. They all brought different customs with them, including their own languages and traditions. At one time, both France and Spain had controlled the city. Then, in 1803, New Orleans became part of the United States. Native Americans and African Americans had lived there for some time. Soon thousands of U.S. citizens, as well as people from other countries, began to move there, too.

One reason so many people went to live in New Orleans was that it sat at the mouth of the Mississippi River. People from all over the world used the river as a trade route. It was usually possible to find work there. Even so, people with darker skin faced **discrimination.** They usually lived in the poorest neighborhoods, where life could be difficult. Louis Armstrong was born in one of these neighborhoods on August 4, 1901.

Louis's mother, Mayanne, was only 15 years old when Louis was born. Louis's father, Willie Armstrong, left when Louis was just three weeks old. Mayanne did not feel she could care for Louis by herself, so she asked her own mother, Josephine, to take him.

For the next five years, Josephine was like a mother to Louis. She took him to church and taught him to respect others. She taught him right from wrong and punished him when he was naughty. But when Louis was five years old, Mayanne sent for him. She was very sick and needed her young son to care for her and her baby daughter, Beatrice. Louis was sad to leave his grandmother, but he was excited to take his first trolley ride to see his mother.

A sign on the trolley read that the front of the bus was for white people only. Louis couldn't read it, so he sat down on the first open seat he found.

Library of Congress

LOUIS ARMSTRONG WAS BORN IN THE LIVELY CITY OF NEW ORLEANS ON AUGUST 4, 1901. THE CITY'S LOCATION ON THE MIGHTY MISSISSIPPI RIVER BROUGHT PEOPLE FROM ALL OVER THE WORLD TO LIVE THERE.

A black woman yelled at Louis to join her in the back. Louis thought she was playing games and didn't obey. She had to pick him up and carry him to the back of the trolley. That was Louis's first experience with **segregation** laws that separated black people from whites.

Louis's new neighborhood was poorer than where he had lived with his grandmother. It was a part of town where people went to gamble and drink alcohol. It was a dangerous place to grow up— so much so that people called it "The Battlefield." Many of the children who lived there had no shoes, even though there were bricks, glass, and nails all over the streets. Most of the time, the families ate red beans and rice because those foods were the cheapest.

©Louis Armstrong House and Archives/Queens College/CUNY

Louis and his family shared a cramped, one-room house with his Uncle Isaac, who had a wife and five children. Louis, his mother, and his sister lived on the left side of the house. His uncle's family lived on the right side. Louis's father lived close by, but he had a new family and never visited his son.

When Louis was six years old, he began attending the Fisk School for Boys. He learned to read and write, but he didn't attend classes regularly. He had a lot of responsibilities as a young boy, and he didn't have much time for school. Louis helped feed his family by going through garbage cans behind restaurants and hotels. He picked out food that wasn't yet spoiled. The family would cut rotten parts from the food, sell some of it, and eat the rest.

After age five, Louis lived in a one-room house in the neighborhood shown at left. His father had abandoned the family, and Louis lived with his mother and sister.

Louis soon had a regular job. At about age six, he began working for the Karnofsky family. The Karnofskys were Russian-Jewish **immigrants** who owned a junk business. Louis helped the Karnofskys buy clothing and coal during the day. After an evening break, he helped them sell the coal to people in the neighborhood.

There were clubs called **honky-tonks** all over Louis's neighborhood. People played many kinds of music in the honky-tonks. Louis loved all of it. He especially liked a new kind of music called **ragtime.** Musicians who played ragtime **improvised,** composing music as they played. It was exciting and fun to hear. In later years, people would say that ragtime helped create yet another new kind of music—**jazz.**

Louis spent a lot of time standing outside of the honky-tonks, listening to the music. He especially enjoyed listening to Joseph "King" Oliver. Oliver played the cornet in a popular band led by trombonist Kid Ory. A cornet is similar to the trumpet in look and sound but is slightly smaller. Louis thought Oliver was the greatest cornet player in New Orleans. He began to dream of being a musician, too.

Louis found his way into the world of music by forming a street-corner singing group with his friends. The group walked down the streets, singing until someone requested a song. People would give the boys small tips in exchange for a few songs. Many of Louis's friends began to call him "**satchel** mouth." They claimed his mouth was so big, it resembled a satchel, a small bag used to carry clothes or books.

Usually, Louis gave his mother any money he earned. But one day, he wanted to buy his first cornet. With the help of the Karnofskys, he bought one at a pawnshop for $5. Louis had talent. He could listen to a song and then imitate it on his horn. This is called "playing by ear."

When New Year's Eve came in 1912, Louis wanted to celebrate. Many adults in the neighborhood celebrated by firing guns into the air. Louis took a gun from his mother's drawer when he went to meet with his friends. While they were walking down the street, a boy shot his gun into the air. Louis wanted to show off, so he shot his gun into the air, too.

Moments later, a police officer arrested him. Louis spent the night in jail. Then he was sent to a **reform school** called the Colored **Waif's** Home for Boys. It wasn't a bad place to be. African Americans cared for the boys and taught their classes. All the children who lived there learned to cook, clean, garden, and even to do carpentry. The school also had a band, taught by Peter Davis. It was an honor to get into the band. The members were allowed to take special trips outside of the home to play in parades and at picnics. Louis was eager to join the band and listened to them practice. Davis finally let Louis join, though not as a cornet player.

First, Davis let Louis play the tambourine. Louis did so well that Davis soon let him play the drums. Then one day, the bugle player left the Waif's Home. Davis let Louis take over that instrument. Louis loved to play the bugle and practiced whenever he could. Once Louis played it well, Davis let him start playing the cornet.

After a year, Louis's mother wanted him to come home. She worked for a kind white family. She hoped they might help her get Louis out of the Waif's Home. The family asked that Louis be released from the school. Finally, he was allowed to go home—on the condition that he live with his father.

Willie Armstrong had just gotten a good job at the factory where he worked. The director at the Waif's Home thought Willie's income would ensure that Louis had everything he needed. Louis wasn't sure he would like living with his father. After all, he didn't know Willie very well. He had never even met his stepmother or stepbrothers. But he did go to live with them for a short time.

While at the Waif's Home, Louis received musical instruction from the band director, Peter Davis. Louis eventually became leader of the Waif's Home band. Peter Davis is the adult seated in the center, and Louis is circled in the background.

The Jazz Age

Soon after Louis moved in, his stepmother had a new baby. Willie Armstrong decided he couldn't feed four children, so he sent Louis back to live with his mother. Back at his mother's home, Louis needed to help support his family. At just 13 years old, he got a job at a honky-tonk playing the cornet. Unfortunately, he couldn't make much money as a musician. There were more than a hundred bands working in New Orleans at the time. Every one of them hoped to get a "gig," a regular job playing music. There wasn't enough work to go around. To make more money, Louis worked at the C. A. Andrews Coal Company each day, from seven in the morning until five in the evening. Then he played cornet at the club until late at night.

Even though it was difficult to find work, it was an exciting time to be in New Orleans. Jazz music was just beginning to take shape. African Americans had created this form of music right there in Louis's hometown. Like New Orleans itself, jazz was a mixture of different cultures. It combined African and European music styles into something no one had ever heard before. And Louis was there from the beginning.

For about four years, Louis worked at many different jobs. He also had a few regular gigs with Kid Ory. Louis got to play his cornet at dances, picnics, funerals, and parades—but he earned most of his money hauling coal.

In 1917, the city government of New Orleans decided that some of the honky-tonks had become too dangerous and closed them down. Musicians had to start looking for other places to work. Many went to Chicago, another city known for its lively music. But Louis found work in New Orleans, the true home of jazz music.

Louis Armstrong was released from the Waif's Home in 1914. He lived briefly with his father but then returned to his mother's home. He is shown here with his mother (seated) and sister.

After leaving the Waif's Home, Louis began to find work as a musician, performing in New Orleans honky-tonks. But he also delivered coal and sold newspapers to help feed his family.

In 1918, King Oliver decided to make the move to Chicago. Kid Ory asked Louis to take Oliver's place in the band. Louis was honored and accepted the gig. Around that same time, he married his first wife, Daisy Parker. He was 17 years old.

Soon a pianist named Fate Marable noticed Louis. Marable had put together the first "colored band" to play on a Mississippi riverboat. He wanted Louis to join. Louis worked with the band from 1919 to 1921. Usually they played for white audiences on dinner cruises. While playing in Fate Marable's band, Louis learned to read music for the first time. At that time, jazz was gaining popularity around the country. Its lively, energetic sound reflected the way many young Americans lived their lives—so much so that the 1920s are often called the Jazz Age.

In 1919, bandleader Fate Marable hired Louis to perform on riverboats that traveled the Mississippi. Louis is shown here (third from right) with the Fate Marable Orchestra aboard the S.S. *Capitol* in St. Louis, Missouri.

In 1922, Louis and Daisy Armstrong broke up. They hadn't spent much time together while Louis was on the riverboat. When they did see each other, they didn't get along very well. That summer, King Oliver asked Louis to join him in Chicago. This was Louis's first time away from New Orleans. He was proud to move to Chicago to play with Oliver, the musician he admired most.

In Oliver's band, Louis met his second wife, a pianist named Lil Hardin. They married in February of 1924. Lil was well educated. She was also involved in Chicago's music scene and showed Louis all the clubs in town. She encouraged him to leave King Oliver's group so that he could lead his own band one day.

Louis took Lil's advice. He left Chicago to join pianist Fletcher Henderson's band in New York City. He hoped this move would help him become famous. It was probably in New York that Louis first began playing the trumpet, the instrument that would make him famous. He also began singing. Soon Louis was making a name for himself. He played with other bands when he had time. He made recordings with Henderson's band. He also played on recordings with other well-known musicians, including Sidney Bechet, Josephine Beatty, Bessie Smith, and Clara Smith.

In November of 1925, Louis left the Henderson Orchestra and went back to Chicago. Lil asked him to join her band at the Dreamland Club. The club advertised him as "Louis Armstrong, World's Greatest Trumpeter." Leaving New York City didn't slow Louis down. He played at a silent movie theater with Erskine Tate's Orchestra. When the theater closed for the evening, he played with Carroll Dickerson's Orchestra at the Sunset Cabaret.

Louis also began to make albums as the leader of his own groups, the Hot Five and the Hot Seven. The band released his song "Heebie Jeebies" in 1925. It featured Louis singing "scat," a style in which the vocalist sings nonsense syllables along with the music. The recording of "Heebie Jeebies" made the band famous all over the country.

In 1922, Louis (seated at center) moved to Chicago to play with King Oliver's band. While playing with Oliver (shown standing at left), he met pianist Lil Hardin (right). The couple married in February of 1924.

LOUIS (THIRD FROM LEFT) MOVED TO NEW YORK IN OCTOBER OF 1924 TO JOIN FLETCHER HENDERSON'S ORCHESTRA, SHOWN ABOVE, WHICH PLAYED AT THE ROSELAND BALLROOM. WHILE IN NEW YORK, HE MADE HIS FIRST RECORDINGS.

Lil was working with Louis regularly. Even so, the couple grew apart. Louis quit working at Dreamland, and he and Lil began to spend more and more time apart. In 1927, Louis's gigs with Tate and Dickerson ended. He formed his own band, a trio with Earl "Fatha" Hines on piano and Zutty Singleton on the drums. These three musicians enjoyed working together. They even decided to open their own club. Unfortunately, none of them had the experience to run a business. They didn't advertise the new club, so few people came to its opening night. In 1928, Louis and his partners decided to close the club and go their separate ways. But Louis wasn't unemployed for long.

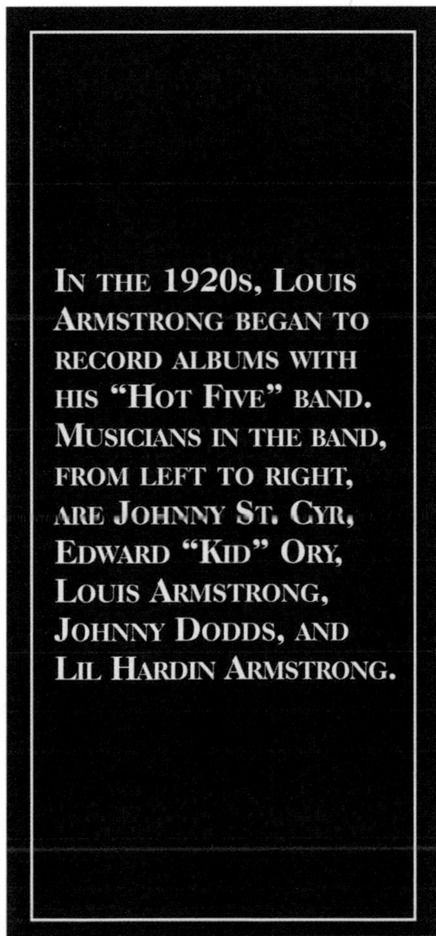

In the 1920s, Louis Armstrong began to record albums with his "Hot Five" band. Musicians in the band, from left to right, are Johnny St. Cyr, Edward "Kid" Ory, Louis Armstrong, Johnny Dodds, and Lil Hardin Armstrong.

©Corbis

Finding Fame

At the end of the 1920s, Carroll Dickerson hired Louis Armstrong to play with his band at Chicago's Savoy Ballroom. These performances were broadcast live on the radio. People all over the country became familiar with Louis's music. He blew his horn with a rich, brassy tone no one had ever heard before. Soon Louis was receiving job offers to perform at parties and dances.

In the meantime, Louis put together another group to make record albums. "West End Blues" was one of the most successful songs recorded at these sessions. In it he played a **solo** that has become one of the most famous in the history of jazz.

In 1929, business at the Savoy began to slow down. The **Great Depression** had begun. Many people were out of work. Few could afford dinner and entertainment at a club like the Savoy. This meant that the owner couldn't afford a band anymore. When Louis had an offer to return to New York and make more recordings, he invited other band members to join him. They got in their cars and started out for the city.

Louis's band soon realized the impact of their radio shows from the Savoy. People recognized them everywhere they went. They had no trouble finding a regular gig at a club called Connie's Inn. In his spare time, Louis played all over New York City. When the band lost its gig at Connie's, he stayed on as a solo act.

Unfortunately, the Depression was growing worse. Many of the glamorous clubs in New York City began to close. Musicians couldn't find work and had to stop playing music. They took jobs doing other things—if they were lucky enough to find work at all.

Louis decided to go to California and try his luck there. His talent and fame quickly won him a yearlong gig at the Cotton Club near Los Angeles.

©Frank Driggs/Archive Photos

Louis (standing in center) played with the Carroll Dickerson jazz band at the Savoy in Chicago. The band's shows were broadcast on the radio and helped to make Louis famous around the country.

The owner of the Cotton Club renamed the band "Louis Armstrong and His Cotton Club Orchestra." Because the club was so close to the movie studios, it attracted a lot of film stars. Louis even appeared in some movies himself.

At the end of his gig at the Cotton Club, Louis returned to Chicago. He continued to work there for many years, without rest. He played with different bands for many kinds of audiences. Louis's trumpet playing was so popular that he received threats from **gangsters** who owned clubs. The gangsters knew that if Louis played at their clubs, his fame would bring large audiences—and a lot of money. Louis and his band had to find a way to get away from these threats. They decided that the best place to go was the South. Just before Louis left, he and Lil separated for good.

In 1931, for the first time in nine years, Louis returned to New Orleans. Blacks and whites alike gathered at the bus station to welcome him to town. Eight bands and a parade were there to greet him. Louis was surprised by his popularity. During his three-month stay, Louis visited the Colored Waif's Home. He donated radios to the boys at the home. He also bought new uniforms for a local baseball team. He gave money to anyone who asked for it.

New Orleans hadn't changed, though. The **racism** Louis had experienced as a young boy was still a problem. This was clear when the band became the first black orchestra to play at the Suburban Gardens nightclub. The event was to be broadcast on the radio, but the owners of the Gardens refused to allow black people in the audience. Louis's black fans had to listen to the music through the club's open windows or on the radio. Even worse, the white radio announcer refused to introduce Louis because he was black. Louis had to introduce himself.

After the band left New Orleans, they made a tour of the South, only to find more racism. It was difficult for them to find hotels that would accept black guests. Many of the clubs where they played would not allow them to use the restroom. The clubs would not even serve food to the band.

©Corbis

During the Depression, millions of Americans were out of work. Musicians had an especially hard time finding jobs, because people could no longer afford to go to nightclubs where the musicians played. Only a fortunate few, like those shown above, could find paying gigs.

The frustrated group headed back to the North. But the gangsters who had threatened Louis earlier were still a problem. In March of 1932, the pressure was too much, and the band broke up.

Louis decided it was time to go somewhere completely different. He had an offer to travel to Europe, and he took it. When he arrived, a reporter called him "Satchmo," a shortened version of his childhood nickname, "satchel mouth."

©Louis Armstrong House and Archives/Queens College/CUNY

Louis opened at a theater called the London Palladium. Every performance was sold out. But the Europeans only knew Louis from his record albums. When they saw him perform live, they didn't like his style of playing. They thought he was too silly and didn't take his music seriously. He also did so much improvising that his songs sounded much different from his records. Many people left his concerts halfway through the performance.

Louis returned home, but he wasn't discouraged. In fact, he was already planning to return to Europe. Many black musicians escaped racism in Europe. Even though racism did exist there, Europeans did not have strict segregation laws like those in the United States. Europe was also a safe distance from the gangsters who threatened Armstrong.

Louis and Lil (center) finally separated in 1931, just before Louis left on his long tour of the South.

©Frank Driggs/Archive Photos

In 1931, Louis and his band traveled to New Orleans to find work. He found that little had changed in the nine years since he had left. Blacks still faced discrimination because of the color of their skin.

©Louis Armstrong House and Archives/Queens College/CUNY

In 1932, Louis traveled to London for the first time. He toured Great Britain from July through November. His first trip was not a great success, but he went back the following year. Soon he was known as "The World's Greatest Trumpeter."

Louis returned to the United States for a short time, working harder than ever. One of the hardest notes for a trumpeter to play is a high C. Louis was able to play anywhere from 250 to 350 high Cs in one song—an amazing feat. He played all the time, at recording sessions, concerts, and radio broadcasts. He worked so hard that he damaged his lip, a serious problem for a trumpet player.

Louis took a short break and then returned to Europe. But his lip injury caught up with him. During a performance in London, his lip split. For the first time in 15 years, he had to take a break. He moved to Paris and relaxed for much of the time that he lived there. Occasionally, he sat in as a guest with jazz groups or played concerts.

Europeans began to admire Louis. A local manager scheduled more concerts for him, but Louis's lip problems returned. When he was unable to perform, his manager took him to court for breaking his **contract**. Louis fled to New York in January of 1935, ready for a fresh start.

LOUIS LOVED TO WRITE. IN FACT, HE WROTE TWO BOOKS ABOUT HIS LIFE: *SWING THAT MUSIC* IN 1936 AND *SATCHMO: MY LIFE IN NEW ORLEANS* IN 1954.

A New Beginning

In the United States, Louis Armstrong spent time recovering from his sore lip and looking for a new manager. He hired a man named Joe Glaser. Glaser was able to take Louis's career to a new level of success. He paid the European manager for the broken contract. He even managed to make the gangsters stop bothering Louis. Glaser was a good businessperson. In the past, Louis had been one of the lowest-paid jazz musicians. With Glaser as his manager, he began making one of the top salaries in the business.

Louis Armstrong soon became the first black person to host a national radio show. He also appeared in more films. Another change for Louis was marrying Alpha Smith in 1938. The two had been dating for a while, and Alpha adored Louis. But Alpha liked to spend money, and she demanded a lot from Louis. The marriage lasted only two years.

During the 1940s, things looked bright for Louis. He married a dancer named Lucille Wilson on October 12, 1942. They moved into a house in Queens, New York. Louis was ready to have a place he could call home. On January 18, 1944, he gave the first jazz concert ever at New York City's famous Metropolitan Opera House.

In 1947, Louis decided to create a smaller band. He called it Louis Armstrong's All Stars. The group was popular for many years, even though it featured both black and white musicians. This was unusual at the time because the United States was still segregated. Some people did not think blacks and whites should even play music together. Even so, the All Stars became one of the most popular jazz bands in the country. By the 1950s, people began to think of Louis Armstrong as the "father of jazz." He had been around since the beginning of jazz and helped shape its future.

©Louis Armstrong House and Archives/Queens College/CUNY

IN JANUARY OF 1935, LOUIS RETURNED TO THE UNITED STATES AFTER TWO YEARS OVERSEAS. HE HIRED A NEW MANAGER, JOE GLASER (SHOWN WITH LOUIS ABOVE), WHO HELPED HIM BECOME MORE SUCCESSFUL THAN EVER.

Louis Armstrong married Lucille Wilson on October 12, 1942. It would be the happiest of his four marriages. He and Lucille stayed together until Louis's death in 1971.

Louis's popularity was at an all-time high just as the **Civil Rights Movement** was gaining ground in the United States. During this time, people fought segregation laws and discrimination. Sometimes other African Americans criticized Louis for not taking part in the struggle for civil rights. Louis thought this was unfair. After all, he had been the first black man to work in places all over the world. He also had formed a popular band with both black and white musicians.

LOUIS MADE MANY WELL-KNOWN MOVIES DURING HIS LIFETIME. HE IS SHOWN HERE (SECOND FROM RIGHT) ON THE SET OF THE 1946 FILM, *NEW ORLEANS*.

Louis took up the hobby of making collages out of newspaper and magazine scraps. They symbolized things that were important to him. Many of his collages featured important African Americans. The one shown here features baseball great Jackie Robinson, the first black man to play major league baseball.

In 1957, Louis proved his dedication to civil rights. He was invited to perform in the Soviet Union on a tour sponsored by the U.S. government. It was an important event, and he was excited to take part in it. But in September, something happened that would keep him from doing so. The Arkansas state government was trying to stop black students from attending a high school in the city of Little Rock. Louis spoke out, saying the federal government should do something to stop the way blacks were treated in the South. He even wrote a letter to President Eisenhower about his feelings.

©Louis Armstrong House and Archives/Queens College/CUNY

When Louis spoke out against the government, he angered some people. The government decided not to send him to the Soviet Union. Instead, a white jazz musician named Benny Goodman was sent on the tour. But the fact that Louis stood up for his beliefs made black Americans gain new respect for him.

Throughout the 1960s, Louis was a popular figure in movies and on television shows. Also, he still toured with the All Stars. He played concerts everywhere from Africa to Asia.

Louis made three tours to Africa in his lifetime and always received a warm welcome. During his visit to the Congo in 1956, he was carried through the streets in a chair before thousands of fans who had come out to greet him.

Armstrong's popular song "Hello, Dolly!" became a number-one hit in 1964. In 1968, he released another hit song called "What a Wonderful World." People around the world loved it.

Louis was the hardest-working entertainer in the United States. He accepted as many gigs as he could. Eventually, the work made him tired. In September of 1968, he had a heart attack. He was losing weight, and his kidneys were failing. His doctor advised him not to play his horn anymore. Louis stopped playing concerts. But in private, he still played his horn quietly, in places where he thought no one would hear him.

In 1969, Louis returned to the hospital with more health problems. He stayed for two months so doctors could perform surgery on his weak lungs. After a lot of rest, Louis was released from the hospital. He continued to perform as a singer, although not nearly as often. As he grew weaker, Louis decided he had to play the horn. It was all he wanted to do in the time he had left.

In March of 1971, Louis made arrangements to play at a New York City hotel, the Waldorf Astoria. His doctor tried to stop him, but Louis was determined to play. After performing there for two weeks, Louis suffered a heart attack and went to the hospital. In June, he was finally sent home. He hoped to recover his strength, but that was not to be. On July 6, 1971, the great Louis Armstrong died in his sleep, shortly before his 70th birthday.

People have honored Louis in many ways since his death. He has been portrayed in statues, songs, and paintings. Postage stamps with his image have been issued all over the world. Schools and awards have been created in his name. Louis Armstrong's hard work and talent made him one of the most respected figures in the history of jazz. Many people consider him to be the most important popular musician of the 20th century. Every jazz musician has listened to Louis's recordings for inspiration, and his legacy lives on in today's music.

Louis never had any children of his own, but he loved kids. He is shown here giving a trumpet lesson to two children from his neighborhood in Queens, New York.

Timeline

1901 Louis Armstrong is born in New Orleans on August 4.

1912 Armstrong is sent to the Colored Waif's Home, a reform school. The following year, he begins playing in the school's band.

1914 Armstrong is released from the Colored Waif's Home. He gets his first gig playing the cornet.

1918 Kid Ory asks Armstrong to take King Oliver's place in his band.

1919 Armstrong begins working with Fate Marable in the first black orchestra to play on a riverboat.

1922 Armstrong joins King Oliver in Chicago.

1924 In October, Armstrong quits King Oliver's band to join Fletcher Henderson's Orchestra in New York.

1925 Armstrong moves back to Chicago to work at the Dreamland Club. He starts work with his two groups, the Hot Five and the Hot Seven. They release a hit record, "Heebie Jeebies."

1928 Armstrong records "West End Blues," on which he plays one of the most famous solos in the history of jazz.

1929 Armstrong moves back to New York and works at Connie's Inn.

1931 Armstrong moves to California to work at the Cotton Club. In June, he goes back to New Orleans for the first time in nine years. There and in other southern cities, Armstrong and his band struggle with racism.

1932 Armstrong goes to Europe and plays at the London Palladium. He becomes known by the nickname "Satchmo." Europeans do not like his playing style on stage, and Louis returns to the United States.

1933 Armstrong injures his lip by working too hard. He takes time off and then returns to London in July. During a performance there, his lip splits. He moves to Paris for a four-month break.

1935 After another lip injury, Armstrong returns to New York City and hires a new manager named Joe Glaser.

1947 Armstrong puts together Louis Armstrong's All Stars, which includes both black and white musicians. The group is popular despite the fact that some Americans do not believe blacks and whites should perform together.

1957 Armstrong speaks out against the U.S. government's decision to stop the integration of a high school in Little Rock, Arkansas. The government then decides not to send him on a special tour to the Soviet Union.

1964 Armstrong's "Hello, Dolly!" replaces a hit song by the Beatles as the number one-song on billboard charts.

1968 Armstrong's song "What a Wonderful World" is popular around the world. He has his first heart attack, and his doctor advises him not to play the trumpet anymore.

1971 In March, Armstrong accepts an offer to play at New York's Waldorf Astoria Hotel. After performing for two weeks, he suffers another heart attack and is hospitalized until June. On July 6, he dies at his home in Queens.

Glossary

Civil Rights Movement (SIV-el RYTZ MOOV-ment)
The Civil Rights Movement was the struggle for equal rights for African Americans in the United States during the 1950s and 1960s. Some black people criticized Louis Armstrong for not playing an active part in the Civil Rights Movement.

contract (KON-trakt)
A contract is a business agreement in which people or companies promise to do certain things. Louis Armstrong's European manager took him to court for breaking a contract.

discrimination (dis-krim-ih-NAY-shun)
Discrimination is the unfair treatment of people simply because they are different. African Americans have suffered discrimination by whites.

gangsters (GANG-sterz)
Gangsters are people who belong to organized groups, or gangs, of criminals. Gangsters threatened Louis Armstrong, hoping he would agree to play in their clubs.

Great Depression (GREAT dee-PRESH-un)
The Great Depression was a period in American history when there was little business activity, and many people could not find work. Jazz musicians had difficulty finding jobs during the Great Depression.

honky-tonks (HONG-kee tonks)
Honky-tonks are cheap nightclubs or dance halls where music is played. Louis Armstrong's New Orleans neighborhood had many honky-tonks.

immigrants (IM-mih-grentz)
Immigrants are people who move to a new country after leaving their homeland. Many immigrants moved to New Orleans in the 19th and 20th centuries.

improvise (IM-pro-vize)
When musicians improvise, they make up music as they play. Jazz musicians often improvise when they perform.

jazz (JAZ)
Jazz is a type of music created in the early 20th century by African American musicians in New Orleans. Jazz is a mixture of African and European music styles.

racism (RAY-sih-zim)
Racism is a negative feeling or opinion about people because of their race. Racism can be committed by individuals, large groups, or even governments.

ragtime (RAG-tym)
Ragtime is a type of music made popular in the late 19th century. Ragtime music has a strong melody combined with an irregular beat.

Glossary

reform school (ree-FORM SKOOL)
A reform school is a place where children are sent when they have done something wrong. Louis Armstrong was sent to a reform school as punishment for firing a gun.

satchel (SATCH-ul)
A satchel is a bag used to carry things. Armstrong's friends nicknamed him "satchel mouth" because his mouth was so big, it was like a satchel.

segregation (seh-greh-GAY-shun)
Segregation is the practice of using laws to separate people from one another. Segregation laws separated blacks and whites in the South for many years.

solo (SOH-loh)
In music, a solo is a song or part of a song played by only one musician. Louis Armstrong's solo in "West End Blues" is considered to be one of the best trumpet solos in jazz history.

waif (WAYF)
A waif is a homeless or neglected child. In 1912, Armstrong was sent to live at the Colored Waif's Home.

Index

Further Information

Books and Magazines

Colier, James Lincoln. *Louis Armstrong: An American Success Story* (Great Achievers). New York: Aladdin Books, 1994.

Gourse, Leslie. *Blowing on the Changes: The Art of the Jazz Horn Players* (The Art of Jazz). New York: Franklin Watts, 1997.

Hughes, Langston. *The First Book of Jazz.* Hopewell, New Jersey: Ecco Press, 1995.

Millender, Dharathula H. *Louis Armstrong: Young Music Maker* (The Childhood of Famous Americans). New York: Simon & Schuster, 1996.

Orgill, Roxane. *If I Only Had a Horn: Young Louis Armstrong.* Boston: Houghton Mifflin Company, 1997.

Sabir, C. Ogbu. *Scott Joplin: The King of Ragtime* (Journey to Freedom: The African American Library). Chanhassen, MN: The Child's World, 2001.

Web Sites

Visit our homepage for lots of links about Louis Armstrong:
http://www.childsworld.com/links.html

Note to Parents, Teachers, and Librarians:
We routinely verify our Web links to make sure they're safe, active sites—so encourage your readers to check them out!